Tai Chi:
Make Tai Chi Internal with 7 Easy Concepts

Yang Wu Chen

© 2019

This document is geared towards providing exact and reliable information in regards to the topic and issue covered. The publication is sold on the idea that the publisher is not required to render accounting, officially permitted, or otherwise, qualified services. If advice is necessary, legal or professional, a practiced individual in the profession should be ordered.

From a Declaration of Principles which was accepted and approved equally by a Committee of the American Bar Association and a Committee of Publishers and Associations.

The information provided herein is stated to be truthful and consistent, in that any liability, regarding inattention or otherwise, by any usage or abuse of any policies, processes, or directions contained within is the solitary and utter responsibility of the recipient reader. Under no circumstances will any legal responsibility or blame be held against the publisher for any reparation,

for use as a source of legal, medical, business, accounting or financial advice. All readers are advised to seek services of competent professionals in the legal, medical, business, accounting, and finance fields.

Contents

Introduction

I have always been puzzled by the fact that Tai Chi is always explained in a philosophical and mystical manner. There are too many theories and principles that do not make much sense to the practitioners. Many of the theories require the practitioner to understand Mandarin to appreciate the meaning. In fact, certain meaning can only be appreciated or understood if the practitioner has a deep understanding of the Chinese culture and tradition. This is a disadvantage for practitioners that are not Chinese. But truth be told, I do see many Chinese practitioners missing the points too. Sometimes I suspect even the master might not really understand the meaning itself. They just made it philosophical to deter the student from asking more questions.

Einstein made a famous quote: "If you can't explain it simply, you don't understand it well enough." I believe that Tai Chi can be imparted in a way that everyone can learn it, regardless of age or physical abilities. We are living in a modern society. We should explain and teach in a systematic and structured manner. This book aims to remove the philosophical and theoretical point of Tai Chi teachings and explains what is required to achieve internal Tai Chi. This book will explain "how to" in a neutral way, regardless of what style or school of Tai Chi one practises.

All concepts are explained in layman's terms. Every topic aims to be short, concise and straight forward. Examples are given to help readers visualize and understand a concept easily. Forms or katas are seldom used as examples so that practitioners of all styles and even other forms of martial artists can understand. I have read too many books that discuss about forms and I usually end up being clueless and confused.

All that said, do note that what I am sharing does comprise of the concepts and theories. Just that I do not want to link them with abstract explanations. Truth be told, it confuses the reader and even myself. I just want things to be clear and simple. Just know that if you are able to understand and achieve what is written in this book, you will be equipped to learn and achieve more advanced skills. Once your body achieves the requirements in this book, it will be easier for you to understand the profound theories and philosophies. And to get your body to achieve what is required, I need to stress the importance of putting in time and effort into practice. This is not a "Get good quick" manual. Good understanding in Tai Chi will not help you in your Tai Chi journey but diligent training will. Without any commitment into practice, the skills will never emerge.

Lastly before we end off, it is highly recommended to find a good master. I did mention that some masters may be deceiving but there is a purpose to finding a good master. This book will help guide you in the right direction without any hocus pocus, but it is unable to see and correct your problem. As practitioners of Tai Chi, we like to feel the practice. It is important to know that feelings can be deceiving, and we may feel "right" even if we are practising it wrong. This is somehow similar to finding directions. You can be very sure that you are facing north but only a compass will tell you the truth. Without a compass, you can still be right but there is a fairly good chance that you are wrong.

A good master need not be highly skilled. Rather, he or she should be able to teach you on the level that you can understand. Often than not, a Tai Chi master can be too high a level. Whatever he is experiencing is something you cannot experience at your level. If you are ever in such a situation, an effective way is to ask the higher-level students as their levels are closer to yours rather than the master. There will be at least one of them who will be able to explain things in a way that you can relate to.

I hope this book will help you accelerate on your learning and get you on the right track. Enjoy!

Chapter 1: What is Tai Chi

Tai Chi or Taijiquan is a martial art that was once, only practised in China but in its current days, practised throughout the world by people of all ages. Tai Chi means "ultimate extreme" as interpreted from its Chinese characters. Tai Chi did not just exist as it is. It is born from Wuji which literally means "no extreme" or "extreme nothingness". The word Wuji is made up of two Chinese characters which each carries their own meaning. Wu means "nothing" and Ji means "extreme". By combining these two characters into a word, it became the two interpretations that were mentioned. Different people may interpret it differently but there are also people that feel that these two interpretations mean the same thing.

Wuji

What is Wuji? Wuji is known to be a void and is totally empty which is what the word "extreme nothingness" means. However, being empty also means that it carries all possibilities. Just like a piece of paper, you can write anything on it. Let us think of this as "totally everything". Now, we see that Wuji can be interpreted as totally empty or totally everything. However, being empty or everything has no form. They are all clumped together and not differentiated which is why we can think of it as "no extreme".

Tai Chi is derived from Wuji. In Tai Chi state, separation and differentiation occurs – yin and yang, hard and soft, good and evil, day and night, man and women, black and white, binary zero and one and so many more. The separations are based on polar opposites. It is also good to note that separation itself is not clear enough and there should be extreme end differences between them, nothing grey and in between. Just like oil and water, they will separate due to their density differences. Even in an emulsion, they will separate eventually. When this principle of "clear separation" is applied into a martial art, we call the martial art Tai Chi.

The Yin Yang Symbol

When anyone discusses about Tai Chi, it is often that the Yin Yang symbol is mentioned. So why is the Yin Yang symbol so important in Tai Chi? Let us start off by defining the Yin Yang symbol. The Yin Yang symbol is basically a circle separated by a black swirling portion and a white swirling portion of equal proportion. The black portion is defined as the Yin and white portion is defined as the Yang. Both Yin and Yang are always equal in quantity but opposite in direction. Yin cannot exist if Yang is not around and vice versa. You need one of them to bring out the other. Who is Yin and who is Yang is also very subjective. To clarify this point, let us use an example. Usain bolt is fast if competing against a human but he will be termed as slow if he is running against a car or a cheetah. Depending on the comparison, it is possible to swing from Yin to Yang or vice versa. A clear separation is compulsory to separate Yin and Yang. Once there is a clear difference, the separation is easily exposed. When there is no clarity, we can think of it as Wuji and once a clear difference is available, we can think of it as Tai Chi. In Tai Chi training, the clear separation is what we are looking for.

To be more detailed, the Tai Chi symbol is not simply just a swirling black and white portion. It is important to note that yang energy is always present within the yin, as represented by the small white circle engulfed in the black. Likewise, the swirling yang energy also contains a seed of black yin energy. The Yin in Yang and Yang in Yin is to show that even in extreme polar differences, the opposite will still exist within. To explain this point, let us imagine an extremely straight man who is muscular and hairy. He is the bread winner and decision maker in the family. He is also arrogant and egoistic. At this point, we can think of this man as someone with high levels of male hormones but scientifically, we know that he will still contain a small portion of female hormones. This is the reason for the seed of opposite energy within the Yin or Yang energy.

Moving on, both Yin and Yang energies are constantly changing and shifting in a cosmic energy dance. Without this shifting, yin and yang cannot separate. Without the separation, yin and yang cannot co-exist. They will revert to Wuji. Through the constant shifting to separate yin and yang, there is Tai Chi. Tai Chi is not just a martial art; it is a philosophy which can be applied to anything. We can apply Tai Chi to our way of lives. We need to clearly separate the things we do. For example, to determine if a matter is urgent, we need to compare it with all the matters on hand before we can decide. The key point here is clear separation. If everything is grey and fuzzy, we will be messy throughout our lives. Of course, Tai Chi principles are actually more profound than these but the above example gives us an idea how we can apply it.

Chapter 2: What is Internal Tai Chi?

As mentioned, Tai Chi is more than martial arts. It is a principle, a philosophy, a concept and a way of life. It can be applied in many things that we do. However, within the context of this book, we are only interested in the martial aspect of it. To be more precise, we are interested to know how to apply Tai Chi in martial arts and more importantly, how to make it internal. Technically, the martial art Tai Chi is internal by nature. Through mass teachings and transmissions, the internal part of it may be lost in translation or forgotten. I will not really call such type of Tai Chi as Tai Chi but rather, think it as an exercise or folk dance. It is still a decent work out that will make us sweat, but it is not that Tai Chi that we as practitioners are really searching for.

A martial art becomes Tai Chi when Tai Chi principles are reflected in its execution. As long as Tai Chi principles are reflected, the martial art is internal. Many schools and masters have their own interpretations. Things like Chi or Qigong used in Tai Chi are termed as internal but this is just one of the avenues practitioners use to achieve "internal Tai Chi". Based on my experience, regardless if you practise Chi in Tai Chi or not, the result will be the same. This is the same as travelling to a place. You can take a boat, a car or a plane. Your journey can be long or short, but everyone will end up at the same place. Therefore, chi or no chi, as long as the art that one practises is based on Tai Chi principles, it is internal Tai Chi.

Now, we have been talking about Tai Chi and making it internal for quite a while. However, what were mentioned do not really give anyone any idea what exactly is internal Tai Chi. So, why does applying Tai Chi principles to a martial art makes it internal? How is external different from internal? What does internal Tai Chi have to do with yin and yang? More importantly, how do we apply that into the martial art? The answer lies with Yin Yang. To be more precise, it lies with separating Yin and Yang.

Splitting Yin Yang

As mentioned in Chapter 1, Tai Chi is born from Wuji. Energies start to move causing Yin and Yang to separate. Yin and Yang need to co-exist. One cannot exist without the other. That means that when Yin appears, Yang is also generated because of Yin's appearance. Strictly speaking, there will not be a situation whereby only Yin or Yang is available. In such a situation, it should be considered as a Wuji state, messy with all possibilities but with no clear differentiations. For Yin and Yang to co-exist, there should be a split or separation. In this case, there will be a clear Yin and Yang appearing together and Tai Chi happens. Let us apply this idea to the Tai Chi moving form. When a form is done without separating Yin and Yang, we term it as an empty form. It does not matter which style or which school that you are practising but if it is empty, it is not Tai Chi and definitely, not internal. The form must consist of both elements of yin and yang simultaneously to exhibit Tai Chi characteristics.

To achieve this, we have to split Yin and Yang within a body. This might sound stupidly obvious but what we are really concerned with is not the Yin Yang. It is the splitting of the Yin Yang that is the key to Tai Chi. As you may recall, the main Tai Chi principle is a "clear separation" of Yin and Yang. If we cannot split the Yin and Yang apart clearly, we will be in a Wuji state. Yin Yang itself cannot exist if they are not split. Now, the idea of splitting Yin Yang is simple but the ability to split yin and yang is awkward as it is not a usual human body movement and we can only achieve it through deliberate and conscious training. This will take many years as it takes time to break the usual habitual movements and build new movements. Finally, when the body achieves that ability to split Yin and Yang, we say that the body has evolved or is reconstructed.

Now let us get a little technical. How do we apply a Yin Yang split to the martial art? Let us study this using the example of punching. To punch with the right fist, it is only natural to pull back the left elbow. The pulling back of the left elbow helps with balancing the throwing out of the right fist. Such a complementing action ensures that the punch is minimally restricted, and the body remains in balance. To make the punch stronger, the body can rotate along with these actions.

The action of punching with the right hand and pulling back the left elbow to complement the punch is a very rough and simple representation of a Yin Yang split. The Yin Yang split is definitely much more than this, but it gives us an idea of what a Yin Yang split is. A Yin Yang split needs to separate two balanced forces that counter each other. In Tai Chi, an ideal Yin Yang split can occur anywhere in the body and does not really require an opposite force in vectored opposite directions. As a matter of fact, the split can occur between a stationary point relative to other moving body part. For example, imagine a person opening a rotating door that is equipped with the auto close mechanism. This will give the door pushing action some resistance. Some people might open the door by pushing off with their rear foot. This uses the power of the leg and whole body to push open the door which is quite an efficient action. To open the door with a Yin Yang split, a person needs to stand still and push the door. The body does not move, only the hand. In this situation, the body is the stationary point and the hand is the moving body part. This is a Yin Yang split. The door is actually also doing a Yin Yang split. The hinges are the stationary point and the door itself is the moving part. Now, this may seem like a Yin Yang split is nothing special but do note that there should be many Yin Yang splits occurring in an action. It really depends on the situation. Let's talk about pushing the door again. Another Yin Yang split can happen between the hand and the rear foot. The hand moves forward to open the door, the rear foot is stationary, the action is balanced. There are many other types of splitting and again, it depends on the situation. However, by understanding this principle and with adequate training, the body will automatically split the required number of Yin Yang within the body when the situation arises.

Chapter 3: Chi and Tai Chi

Internal Tai Chi is about splitting Yin Yang. To split Yin Yang, the body must be reconstructed. As mentioned previously, some schools like to associate internal Tai Chi with the internal energy known as "chi". This energy allows the practitioner to heal their illnesses and strengthen their body. It can be transmitted to any body part to strengthen it for striking or withstand a hit. It can also be circulated inside the body to increase the vitality. A high-level qigong practitioner can even project the chi out of the body to heal or control another person. These are the mysterious miracles of chi. As you can see, I am a firm believer of chi but at the same time, I believe that you do not need chi to reconstruct the body and split Yin Yang.

I started my training in Yang style Tai Chi and focused heavily on directing the chi around the body. I must say that chi training in Tai Chi has definitely helped me to understand what Tai Chi is better and I used to believe that internal Tai Chi deals with chi. Tai Chi styles that do not practise chi is not internal Tai Chi. However, in my journey of Tai Chi practice, I have also noticed other practitioners exhibiting Tai Chi abilities without even knowing how to feel chi. They are taught only to take note of their structure and movements in their form. This leads me to see Tai Chi from another perspective. Although we can use chi to train the body to reconstruct, it is also possible to reconstruct the body without the use of chi. Now, here comes the sweet part. Once the body has been reconstructed, chi will flow even if you do not train chi. The truth is chi and body reconstruction come hand in hand. A practitioner that trains using chi is aware of chi and will be able to control chi. For a practitioner that does not train with chi, he will start to notice chi movement when the body starts reconstructing but he may not know how to use or control it.

Most schools or styles of Tai Chi that claims to be internal generally incorporate qigong into their practices, but we have to be clear that Tai Chi is not qigong. There are many qigong schools but as long as they do not follow Tai Chi principles, they are not Tai Chi but just simply a qigong practice.

Practising Chi wrongly

One of the frequent questions that is frequently heard is "Will chi damage our body if practised wrongly?" There are people out there who are concerned that if the chi is directed in the wrong way, the practitioner may go mad or the body will suffer damage from chi implosion. I believe that such thoughts are likely due to the influence of Chinese Kung Fu movies. In the movies, the practitioner tried to break through to the final level of the ultimate kung fu but got distracted and ended up suffering internal injuries. To signify this point, the practitioner would usually throw up blood from the mouth and went into a coma or end up in a very weak state. I used to love such movies but as my Tai Chi journey progresses, such movies seem really hilarious to watch. To be honest, I have never seen anyone suffered internal injuries due to qigong practice. Actually, the main problem of qigong is that practitioners are not practising enough. There are too many distractions in the current age that reduce the commitment levels of practitioners. People usually want fast results and after a month of weekly classes, they think that they are better off in the gym. Therefore, the real danger is really not chi implosion but rather, lack of training. However, it should be noted that being too committed to Tai Chi can actually be a problem. Having passion for what you do is definitely good but when it becomes an obsession, that is where the problem begins. From a personal experience, there was a time when I lost sleep and concentration due to Tai Chi obsession. The brain kept thinking about how to break the code of Tai Chi and would not stop. I just could not come to a logical conclusion on how Tai Chi works. Finally, I managed to get out of this misery by diligently training the form and not being bothered about what I am doing. From where I come from, there is a phrase that says, "Too much analysis gives you paralysis". It is important to note that sometimes we do not have enough knowledge to understand certain things. We should let it be if this is the case. With enough time and practices, we will be able to understand or have a breakthrough as time passes. This situation is not solely for Tai Chi but basically applies to every hobby or things that we do.

Another danger concern to be aware of is actually over practising. Tai Chi is about being in balance. Remember that if there is Yin, there will also be Yang in equal amount. Therefore, there should be a balance between training and resting. Training too much without adequate rest will damage the body rather than enhancing it. To reconstruct the body, the quality of the training is actually more important than the quantity of the training. Therefore, it is important to practise the part of the form that you are weak in. There is no need to practise the full form diligently every single day. You may extract a part of the form and just drill on it. If the action is done correctly, the body should get tired after a few practices as all the sleeping muscles and tendons are activated and put to work. However, this only applies to non-beginners. Training for beginners should always start from quantity so as to get familiarised with the moving form. After numerous trainings, the practitioner will start to understand the points to train and the training should then be changed from "quantity" to "quality" type of training.

Chapter 4: The Tai Chi Body

Again, Tai Chi is about reconstructing the body to split Yin Yang. By applying Tai Chi principles to any form of martial arts, it makes that martial art Tai Chi regardless if the form looks like it. For example, Judo is well known for its throws which is quite different from Tai Chi. However, Judo can be considered as Tai Chi if it splits Yin Yang to execute the throw. The real question is how to apply Tai Chi principles into the martial arts when their styles are so different from the Tai Chi we practise? Each martial art has its own principles and theories to follow and applying Tai Chi principles to these martial arts will likely contradict some of the moves. This is very true so let's not force Tai Chi principles onto other martial arts.

To apply Tai Chi to other martial arts, the secret is to have a Tai Chi body. A practitioner who has trained Tai Chi for a long time should assumedly has a very well reconstructed body. The body has the ability to split Yin Yang very precisely and if he is forced to train some other martial arts like boxing, it is likely that the punches will split Yin Yang as well since the body has already been trained to do that.

To illustrate this better, let us discuss more about the reconstructed body. The concept of a reconstructed Tai Chi body is in fact, a very simple one. The body just has to behave like sand. We know that it is easy to push an object with a fixed shape as every point on the object is connected together as one whole piece. When any part of the object moves, the rest of it has to follow. However, it is easier to push sand. Yes, it is easier to push sand. The part of the sand that is pushed will move easily but here is the contradiction. The rest of the remaining sand will remain behind unaffected by the push. Relating back to the human body, the balance of the person being pushed will not be disrupted if only the part that is pushed moves along with the push while the main balance of the body remains stationary. In this way, the stability of the person is maintained and unaffected by the push, just like the sand. However, an untrained human body cannot behave like sand. The body tends to tense up to obstruct the push from an opponent, just like a fixed shape object. To make the body behaves like sand, the rest of the body have to split their connection from the part being pushed. The rest of the body will look stationary but as a matter of fact, it has to move to compensate for the part that is being pushed by the opponent. The compensating movements are internal which are hard to notice through the naked eyes. Such internal movements are also the reason that Tai Chi is well, internal! When the moves are internal, there are very minimal movements but very effective to dissolve the attack from the opponent since the opponent is unable to feel anything.

To achieve the internal movements, the chest has to sink while the back stretches, the shoulder has to be pressed downwards, the kua has to rotate, sending the energy to spiral down the foot and into the ground. Such movements are extremely hard to feel or detect and thus, the non-Tai Chi opponents will have a tough time understanding why they cannot keep their balances. If it is difficult to detect, it is difficult to react. This is one of the reasons why it is so hard to apply strength on a real Tai Chi master. All attacks will be deflected away or directed into the ground. With the internal movements, even if the opponent sees or anticipates an attack, the opponent will have a challenging time dodging as he cannot feel and react to the attack. This is like someone attacking you with an invisible weapon. You can see the attack coming but you do not know how big or how long the weapon is. You cannot tell if it is a sword or an axe or even a gun. Therefore, it is easy to get hit. As long as you have no idea what it is and how it hits you, you cannot block or dodge it and will end up falling for the hit most of the time.

Now, we have briefly talked about making the body behave like sand and also having internal movements. You might have noticed that such movements require the body to have separated movements. Such actions are also a concept of splitting Yin Yang. Of course, there are more details to split Yin Yang properly but what we need to know now is that Yin Yang is split when your body disconnects itself to perform different actions.

Once the body is reconstructed adequately, any moves and techniques executed should have the effect of Yin Yang splits and thus the emphasis on how a move or technique is executed becomes unimportant. What we should aim for is the Tai Chi body, not the techniques. The Tai Chi journey is an endless reconstruction of the body. You start off as a fixed shape object. By training, you break the fixed shape object into two parts. With more training, you break the two parts into four parts and so on until your body becomes sand. Even if the body becomes sand, you can train to become powder. There is no end to it. By breaking down the body, there will be a day whereby any part of the body can deflect or attack the opponent. There is no need for a palm strike or a punch. You can attack using your back or even your tummy. I have actually seen a master using his armpit to deflect an opponent during a closed-door demonstration, but I am sure that anyone in the right state of mind will never attack the armpit. Anyway, what we can see here is that we train to disconnect the body into very fine parts. This is the state that we are trying to achieve and the closer we are to this state, the better we can split Yin Yang.

Chapter 5: 7 Concepts to Make Tai Chi Internal

The following information is a list of training concepts that I used in my Tai Chi journey. If I had this information shared with me when I started out, I will have definitely spent shorter time to get to where I am. I am going to share this information with you now and hope that you do not waste time trying to figure out what is going on in your Tai Chi journey. Do note that it is not necessary or even possible to train all the items mentioned below simultaneously. There are many requirements from Tai Chi and to achieve all of them, we need to train each requirement one by one. Once you have gotten hang of a concept, then start on another.

Concept 1: Intent

This may not be the first time you are hearing this but "intent" is really something very crucial in Tai Chi. In Chinese character, intent is pronounced as "Yi". Intent or "Yi" in Tai Chi is something that is abstract and intangible but that does not mean that it is something very complex. To make it simple, let us think of intent as the driver of the moves in the Tai Chi moving form. This means that we use intent to move our body. For example, if I want to move my hand to touch my nose, I'll imagine and feel that my hand moves by its own to touch my nose without my muscles moving. This is the general gist of it. In another example, we can imagine and feel that we are very heavy as if all of our weights have flowed down to the legs. If we imagine hard enough, the body will likely move by itself and adjust the weight to feel heavy on the legs. We use intent to drive all our moves. It is important that we start all our moves with intent, and then the body will move accordingly with the intent. With enough training and practice, what the mind perceives, the body will execute.

If you have noticed the examples above, we use intent by imagining the action and feeling the action. However, the first requirement to use intent is to actually believe in it. Tai Chi is not just a training of the body; it is also the training of the mind. We need to have a strong mind to balance a strong body. This is also a concept of Yin Yang separation. The intent drives the physical movement but still is clearly separated. When the intent appears, the body moves. When the intent disappears, the body stops moving.

I like to imagine intent as water flowing through my body. I try to feel it flowing through the body as if my body is made up of pipes and hoses. When the intent goes down the leg, the leg feels like water flowing from the thigh all the way to the toes and into the ground. Do note that the intent is not limited to stay within the body. It needs to be projected out of the body whenever required. The intent has to be projected as far as you can see or imagine and can be projected from any part of the body. Intent projected out of the body should never be short or near. Intent is limitless. It should go as far as your mind can stretch it.

Some practitioners like to think that the intent is Chi but intent and Chi is technically different. Intent is basically a thought generated by the mind while Chi is a type of energy. There is a phrase in Tai Chi that says, "intent arrives, chi arrives". Intent leads the action, it also leads the chi. In practice, it does not matter if you can tell the difference between intent and Chi. As long as you imagine and feel the moves, you are training both intent and chi simultaneously.

Concept 2: Structure

A Tai Chi training is usually about being relaxed and soft, but it is also important that the body maintains a good structure. Our body is just like a building. A building with a good structure will not topple easily during intense winds and earthquakes. To make the building stronger, we can equip it with shock absorbing materials. Any external impact onto the building will be greatly reduced and not affect the structure of the building. Similarly, by behaving like sand with a good body structure, we can easily keep our balance. On the other hand, a bad structure with a body of sand will still easily succumb to attack. That is also one of the reasons why a small Tai Chi master can easily throw a big guy. The master breaks the opponent's structure and can easily defeat the opponent even if the opponent is soft and relaxed. A good structure is not difficult to achieve but difficult to maintain once we keep moving. This is why we need to train diligently to make the body remember the structure between movements. Below, we will discuss about a few essential points of a good structure. Once the body is trained to keep these points, the structure will naturally be maintained. There are two parts to a proper structure, the upper body and the lower body. The upper body refers to the tummy and above. The lower body refers to the pelvis and below.

Upper Body

The requirements to lift up the head, tuck in the chin, sink in the chest while stretching the back and tuck in the tail bone (coccyx) is a very common structure theory for Tai Chi. This concept is also widely used in Chinese kung fu. The Russian martial arts "Systema" also emphasises in keeping the tail bone tuck in. Keeping the tail bone tuck in will enable the chi to be held in the "dan tian". The dan tian is located around two to three fingers below the navel inside the human body. It acts as a reservoir and as well as a pump for the chi, similar to the function of the heart to move the blood. If the tail bone is not tuck in properly, the chi will not hold well and is easy to dissipate. This is how the schools that believe in chi will explain. However, the chi theory might not be easy for everyone to comprehend. Let us take a look at this concept from another perspective. The dan tian coincidentally happens to be also our centre of gravity. The idea of the structure is to keep our balance neutral, not towards the front nor the back. To make things simple for the practitioner, just know that the spine has to be stretched, that is all. Basically, the top of the head and the tail bone have to act like they are pulled in opposite directions, with the head going upwards and the tail bone going downwards. The tail bone is technically pulled downwards rather than being tucked in. The normal relax position of the tail bone is usually pushed outwards like a "perky ass". By tucking the butt in, the tail bone should theoretically face downwards. With the tail bone tucked in the right angle, the connection of the feet and the hands can be achieved. When the connection is achieved, the push of the hand will reach the feet. This is what it means by "borrowing strength from the ground". Do note that making the connection will not make you more rooted to the ground. How rooted you are is relative to the opponent. The connection is just to close the loop for the push or pull to reach the ground. As for the head, it is necessary for the chin to try to touch the neck when stretching the head up. This will prevent the head from extending forward instead which is a common problem in the modern society. Too many hours behind the computers have made our necks stretched forward. We think that our heads are straight but take a moment to look into the mirror to confirm this point. What we think and what we really are doing can be quite different. As for the requirement of the chest, it should sink down. This will cause the back to open and stretch forward. Based on experience, it is very difficult to do all these actions together. A straightforward way will be to focus on an action first like tucking in the tail bone. Once the action is fixated, train another body part.

Lower Body

Anyone that practises Tai Chi should have a good control over their kua. The kua can be thought of as the joint between the pelvis and the thigh bone. It is one of the largest joints in the body and has a wide range of motions. In Tai Chi, we like to use the term "open the kua". To open the kua literally means to well, open it. The usual position of the kua is closed. When we are sitting on a chair, it is closed. When we are walking, it is closed. The kua is closed most of the time and thus we lose control over it after some time. There are many people who cannot open their kua. Embarrassingly, I used to be one of them. I do not even know that the kua can move. To know if you can move or open the kua, you just have to turn your body without the knee following. If the knee turns in the direction that your body is turning, the kua is not opened. By training the kua properly, it is possible to keep the knee from moving when the body turns. To keep the knee from turning, the kua has to push the leg downwards into the ground. If the knee keeps moving during the Tai Chi practice, it is easy to get the knee injured. If you noticed, turning the body while keeping the knee from moving is splitting Yin Yang. Technically, there is a separation of intent from the kua, one goes down the leg, the other turns the body.

Concept 3: Split up the body

Using intent, we can "split" the body into separate segments. Once these segments are clearly formed, the body will be able to split Yin Yang. The splitting of the body is achieved by generating separate intents into different directions while training the form. Having a few intents at the same time can be quite taxing for the mind and not easy for beginners. However, with practice it should become a second nature in time to come. As a start, there should be two intents. They should be balanced meaning the intent should be simultaneous and equal. Both are generated at the same time, equal in intensity and same amount of time. When one intent starts, the other must exist. When one cease, the other disappears. This is the same as Tai Chi being born from Wuji. If separating two intents at the same time is too taxing, it is okay to generate one intent first, finish it then generate the second intent. With enough practice, generating two intents together should not be too taxing. Once you are able to generate two intents, you can try to generate more. The more intents you can split, the better your skills will be. We will discuss the major body segments that we can split into but as the skill progresses, splitting segments of the body will increase and becomes more obvious. The ideal requirement is to split the body into so many fine segments that the body becomes sand. That is how our bodies get reconstructed.

Separate the top and bottom

The intent starts from the waist and splits into two. One goes up to the head, into the sky and the other goes down to the legs into the ground. The feeling is like the head is tied up by a string and hanging while the lower body is sinking into the ground. You may feel that you are stretching the spine while doing so. Take note to tuck in the chin to ensure that the head is not popping forward. This exercise will help to improve your rooting. You can train this in both stationary form and moving form.

Separate the limbs

The intent that moves through the body should be smooth and detailed. It should not jump to the next body part abruptly. For example, the intent of the arm starts from the shoulder, to the elbow, to the wrist, through the fingers, out of the body and projected far away. The intent should not go from the shoulder straight to the fingers. The check points are usually the joints but make sure to let the intent move through the arm between the joints too. For the legs, the intent should start from the kua, through the thigh, the shin, the ankle, the foot and into the ground.

Separate the torso

For the torso, the intent can move along the front, back or the whole torso. If the intent travels on the back, the feeling is on the spine. If the intent is on the front, it travels along the tummy and chest. If the intent is on the whole torso, I like to imagine water feeling up the torso or flowing down the torso, depending on the direction of the intent.

Separate the arm and body

This is a good training to improve your rooting when pushing an opponent. The intent separates into two from the shoulder. One intent goes through the arm and the other goes down the body into the ground. Without this training, the body tends to move forward along with the push. The opponent will take this opportunity to pull you and there will be a good chance of falling. However, if the separation of the arm and body is clear, the opponent will still pull your arm but will not be able to get your balance. This concept applies for striking too. If the separation is not clear, the body will move forward when striking instead of sinking down.

Concept 4: Intent into the ground

This is the secret to Tai Chi "Thousand pound drop" or why Tai Chi masters feel heavy. The idea is to behave like an iceberg. The tip of the iceberg is merely a fraction of what is underneath the water. The opponent can see or feel the "tip" but they will not know the danger of what is underneath until they are hit.

To achieve this iceberg effect, we need to send the intent down the body and into the ground. The concept of sinking into the ground is usually for striking. When we strike, we will send an intent out from the body part that is attacking and another intent down the body into the ground. This will ensure that we are stable and yet powerful like the iceberg. However, we can also tweak this concept into "connecting to the ground" if we are receiving the attack. This skill is commonly known as rooting. Any incoming threat from the opponent can be neutralized quickly by directing it into the ground. The opponent will feel that he is dealing with a mountain or a deeply rooted tree. All the attacks will make him feel that he is powerless because he is dealing with Mother Earth herself!

A good structure complements a good rooting. It is rather difficult to explain the details in text but there is a good exercise to get a good rooting with good structure - Just push the wall! Find a wall, maintain an upright posture and separate two intents. One through the arms and the other down the body. The feeling of this exercise is like stretching the body from the back and into the arm. The legs should not push but sink down as much as the back stretches.

Sending the intent into the ground is in fact a very important skill in Tai Chi. Most of the moves in the moving form are supposed to have an intent into the ground. This skill is almost like salt in food. We need to use it all the time. You can give up learning chi or being soft but sending the intent down the ground is the absolute skill we need to master. The better we can do this, the more stable we are. That is all that matters.

Concept 5: Open up the Joints

The joints are the connecting parts of the body and they affect the movements of our body. By opening up the joints, we aim to increase the mobility and range of the body parts. A good indication of an opened joint is separate movements. For example, try turning the head to look over your shoulder. Does the torso turn together with the head even by a tiny little bit? Does the shoulder hunch forward as you try to look over the shoulder? These are signs of a closed joints. Most of us have these issues. In Tai Chi, we aim to separate each body part so that we can split Yin Yang. If the joints are closed and locked, Yin Yang cannot be separated with clarity. We train to make every part of the body perform their own independent actions as if they are not linked together. That is why our bodies are reconstructed when we train Tai Chi.

The secret to opening up the joints is to simply to stretch and twist them. The stretch and twist can happen throughout the moves but for training purpose, you can try to stretch at the end of every moves. For example, after you have completed the move "single whip", stretch your both arms out as far as possible before moving on to the next move. When stretching and twisting, we need to project the intent far and away as if it is pulling us. Try to stretch and hold for a few seconds before moving to the next move to make the stretching effective. Stretching and twisting is an isometric exercise and isometric exercises train the tendons. Once the tendons are trained to be strong and flexible, the joints will naturally be opened. However, tendons are tough fibers that are hard to train. It may take a long time to fully develop them. But once they are trained, they retain their strength longer than muscles do. This is why Tai Chi focuses on training the tendons. As a start, we aim to train the major joints like the kua and the shoulders. As training progresses, the other joints like elbows and wrists have to be trained too. Below, we will discuss about them.

Shoulder, elbow, wrist and fingers

The shoulder is a ball and socket joint. It has a wide range of motions, but it is also one of the stiffest joints. To train the shoulder joint, stretch out both arms to the sides like they are pulling the body apart. At the same time, press the shoulder down towards the ground. This exercise actually stretches all the joints in the arm, including the elbow and wrist. This exercise can be done whenever you are free. It can last for a few seconds to a few minutes. Depends on how much time you have and how long you can withstand the stretches in your joints. While doing the exercise, it is important to spread out the fingers. This will ensure that the fingers are properly stretched too. The fingers should not be loose and relaxed. The objective is to open up the joints, not to train to be relaxed and soft. With enough training, it is possible to gain small control over the joints and slightly elongate them at will. Elongation of the joints is a crucial skill for internal Tai Chi.

Kua, knee, ankle and toes

The kua is amongst the biggest joints in the human body and it is the secret of Tai Chi. It has the ability to produce tremendous power if properly trained. It is also one of the main body parts to produce the internal movement. To know if we trained the kua well, simply stand with the feet shoulder width apart and turn your body to the left. If the kua is opened, both knees will remain straight and not turn with the body. Actually, to turn the body left, the right leg actually pushes down into the ground and make the kua open towards the left, thereby turning the body. Notice that there is actually a Yin Yang split when the leg pushes down while the body turns. The split starts at the kua. One intent goes down the leg, the other goes to the opposite shoulder. E.g. right leg, left shoulder.

When the intent goes down the leg, the knee and ankle try to elongate and pushes into the ground. The toes are clenched as if they are trying to grip onto the ground tightly. While trying to open up the kua, it is very easy to injure the knee. Here are a few points to note so that the knee are well taken care of. Firstly, make sure that the knee does not wobble left and right. Secondly, the knee should also not be bent past the foot and toes. Ideally, the shin should be vertically straight up to the knee but that might be a very tough requirement to achieve from a practical point of view.

Concept 6: Every move is a stretch or compression

In Tai Chi, we need to execute all our moves by stretching and compressing. If the move is neither stretched or compressed, we term the move as "loose". A "loose" move does not train our joints and tendons. Also, intent projection should always be used for stretching and compressing. Remember that the intent is the driver of all our moves. The stretch or compress can happen at any point throughout the body. For example, imagine that the arm is hanging relaxed by the side of the body. To lift the arm up, press the shoulder down and feel the arm floating up like pumping helium or hydrogen into it. As the training progresses, the arm will feel lighter and floats up faster. The more you train, the better the feeling gets, the finer the movement becomes.

Now, if the arm is lifted to horizontal shoulder level, the shoulder cannot compress to lift the arm anymore so instead, we stretch it like our hand is being pulled. When we stretch or compress our moves, we need to stretch and compress another body part to balance the force. For example, when we stretch out the arm horizontally, there should be an equal compression down the body. Such a movement is splitting Yin Yang.

Once we are comfortable to compress and stretch our movements, we need to include spirals into them. As much as possible, we should twist and rotate our arms and bodies in conjunction with the stretch or compression. Once our body can compress, stretch and spiral freely throughout the moves, we have acquired the spiral silk reeling energy.

To make the stretching and compression more effective, all the moves should be exaggerated and stretched as much as possible. For example, the shoulders, elbows, back, spine and kua should be stretched as if they are trying to detach from the body. Any part of the body that feels tensed or sore should be intentionally stretched and pulled until the tightness loosens up. Such a training might make the Tai Chi moves look ugly and off, but they are compulsory. Take for example, if you want to straighten a rolled-up paper, will you pull the paper straight or will you roll the paper in the other direction? I will definitely roll the paper in the other direction. Exaggerating the stretch and compression is using the same concept. However, do note that exaggerating the moves are only for training purpose to open up the stiff joints faster. Once the joints are loosened, do return to normal practice range.

Concept 7: Magnets on your body parts

Another point to improve your Tai Chi is to make all your moves move like there is a magnetic field in between. To illustrate this point, let's use a punch as an example. Imagine that there is a magnet on your fist and another magnet with the same polarity on your forehead. When the punch is thrown out, the head and fist will "pull themselves apart". This is also another example of Yin Yang split in Tai Chi. We can also have magnet points with different polarity. This is for moves that are closing in. For example, in a horse stance, we can imagine that magnets are pulling one leg to another. As you might have noticed, the Tai Chi moves take reference from a body part and moves towards or away from it. As the training progresses, we should have many of such magnet reference points together and this will help us to maintain the structure and balance the force. By balancing the dynamic forces in the body, we can preserve our balance.

Chapter 6: Better health

When people practise Tai Chi, they are basically looking for health or martial skill. And as age catches up, people prefer health over martial skills. However, why is Tai Chi good for health? Some say it is good for balance and some say it is because of the chi circulating in the body. If we look at what we are training, we can find some logical explanation to this. By training our bodies, we are mainly opening up the joints and stretching the tendons. Once the joints are opened up and the tendons are trained, the "passages" in the body open and the chi will flow better. As we age, the joints stiffen up and we lose our flexibility. As flexibility decreases, the range of movement falls. Once the range of movement gets limited, we tend to move less. And as we move less, the chi and blood cannot flow that well. In such a case, the health deteriorates, and life slowly trickles away.

Opening the joints increase the flexibility and strength of the tendons. The blood will flow better and the toxic in the body can efficiently be transported out from the body. This is quite the same reason as per normal exercises. The difference here in Tai Chi is that we are training the tendons more than the muscles.

What was mentioned is basically more of a layman logical kind of explanation. From a scientific perspective, studies have shown that Tai Chi has a wide range of positive benefits on overall health and well-being like increased strength and flexibility, lowered blood pressure and enhanced immune function. Different practitioners may experience different health benefits, but we shall discuss the common ones that one may experience.

Balance control and falls

Studies have shown that continual Tai Chi training (between 8 and 16 weeks) improves balance, flexibility and knee strength, and reduces the incidence of falling in the elderly. Three cross-sectional studies found that long-term Tai Chi practitioners had greater flexibility in the lower extremities than non-practitioners, and that Tai Chi improved one's manner of walking.

Cardiovascular and respiratory systems

Elderly patients who practised Tai Chi at least four times a week for a year exhibited enhanced cardiorespiratory function, strength and flexibility compared with a control group. Another study reported that long-term tai chi practitioners had higher oxygen uptake rates and lower body fat percentages than their less active counterparts.

Musculoskeletal conditions

One randomized but controlled trial of osteoarthritis patients reported that practising Tai Chi for twelve weeks resulted in improved arthritis symptoms, decreased tension, and greater satisfaction with general health. A non-randomized study suggested that Tai Chi could improves muscle strength and endurance in the knees of elderly individuals. Another study of patients with multiple sclerosis found that subjects who practised Tai Chi experienced improvements in vitality, social functioning, mental health, and the ability to carry out certain physical activities.

Psychological responses

Older adults who participated in a Tai Chi exercise program showed demonstrably better scores on indices that measured depression, psychological distress, and positive well-being. A non-randomized, controlled study, meanwhile, showed that patients with multi-infarct dementia or Alzheimer's disease who participated in twice-weekly tai chi sessions for 7 weeks demonstrated "thinking that was focused and insightful, beyond the level normally manifested for this group of participants."

Hypertension

One randomized, controlled trial found similar reductions in systolic blood pressure between patients practicing Tai Chi and those engaging in regular aerobic exercise. Another study of recovering heart attack patients found reductions in both systolic and diastolic blood pressure levels among those who performed Tai Chi exercises.

We see many benefits associated with Tai Chi practice. However, practitioners with health issues should still consult their physicians and not pin their hopes on Tai Chi alone for a full recovery. Tai Chi is not a panacea to all illness. Despite the health benefits that we have seen, we have to remain realistic and admit that there are some issues that Tai Chi cannot address.

Lastly, I have to stress that it is essential to keep yourself hydrated properly all the time. I know this is obvious, but it is important. Our body is made up of sixty to seventy percent water. Muscle is seventy-five percent water. Fascia which is the tissues that wraps the muscles and organs together has about seventy percent water. Tendon is mainly collagen which water is an intrinsic component to it. Fats and bones have lesser water content, but they are also about ten percent water. With proper hydration, training of the muscles and tendons will give better results. Dried up fibres are hard to stretch and twist. Lastly for the record, drinking coffee or tea is not hydration. You can drink them but never replace water with them. Coffee and tea should only be on top of your daily water intake.

Chapter 7: Why are we doing these in Tai Chi?

This chapter is specially written to help clear some questions that a practitioner has about Tai Chi in some point of the journey. There are some topics that no one specifically explains or touch on. We hope to cover them in this chapter. The topics discussed are short and aims to clear up some questions rather than dwell into the details. Topics like "should we be soft and relaxed" and "why do we train slowly" will be covered in this chapter.

Tai Chi is about being soft and relaxed

Tai Chi must be soft and relaxed. This can be quite a misleading phrase as it makes beginners too relaxed until there is no structure. Often, the definition of being soft and relaxed has not been made very clear to the practitioner and everyone forms their own interpretation. To be soft and relaxed, we need to have the capacity to be soft and relaxed. The capacity here refers to anything that will allow you to be relaxed. For example, if a child is pushing an adult with all his might, do you think the adult can be soft and relaxed? In normal circumstances, the answer will be yes. This is the capacity that we are looking for. So, for us to be soft and relaxed, we need to feel secure and not threatened. And for us to feel that way, the opponent's attack has to be ineffective. For that to happen, we have to be rooted to the ground. If we can direct all the opponent's attack into the ground, we will never feel threatened and can always be soft and relaxed. However, if our balances are taken, we will definitely tense up instead of being soft and relaxed. We will struggle and try to grab anything available to remain in balance.

Now, if we are not soft and relaxed, are we still doing Tai Chi? The answer is yes, as long as we are splitting Yin Yang in our moves. Being soft and relaxed is just a reflection of the Tai Chi skill. However, it is often misunderstood as a requirement of Tai Chi. We can be hard and stiff or even use all our strength in Tai Chi. These is no wrong to it. However, there is a catch to this. To split Yin Yang, we need to disconnect our body parts to perform individual actions. If we can do this, even when we are using strength and being stiff, the reflection is soft and relaxed. Therefore, do not dwell on being soft and relaxed too much. It might actually kill your Tai Chi skills. I have seen many strong practitioners going limp just to be soft and relaxed. They achieve much lesser than they should in the end. The real Tai Chi training talks about refining. That means you start off as a square. Cut off the four corners and you become an octagon. Now you are closer to being a circle. As you cut off more sides, your skills become more refined. What this translate to is we start off Tai Chi with strength and stiffness. The more we train, the more the stiffness we break down, the softer we become. All that said, we should start off as who we are. It is hard to practise Tai Chi when we try to be someone that we are not. If we are strong, we start off strong. If we are soft, we start off soft. The objective is to split Yin Yang, not training to be strong or soft.

Four Ounces overcome a Thousand Pounds

The concept of Tai Chi is to use minimal strength to fight strong opponents. Logically, this is quite unlikely as a small force can never be able to overcome a big one. So, what is the secret behind this? Definitely it is not using soft or redirection of the opponent's attack. Being soft does not work unless you are rooted. Once you are rooted and better balanced than the opponent, you can basically do anything. However, this is only one of the secrets. The next secret is to not take the incoming force head on. I believe many practitioners have this idea to cushion and return the attack back to the opponent. This is ideally the image that people have about Tai Chi which is to use soft and relax to overcome strength. However, the truth is far from this image. To use a small force to overcome a big one, the small force has to come from the side and not head one with the opponent's big force. To visualize this point, imagine a truck running at full speed towards north. The best way to stop the truck is to ram a car into the side of the truck. If the car is to ram head on into the truck, the car will be crushed. If the car is in free gear, lets the truck hit it head on and starts applying brakes. Do you think the car can stop the truck? Likely not! With these scenarios in mind, it is likely that we can accept the idea of using a small force from the side to overcome a big one. Now, here is another secret.

For a small force to be effective over a big force, the small force has to be applied at the same time as the big force. The reason to this is simple. When an opponent pushes you, he is stiff as long as he is pushing or pulling you. The opponent's body has to stiffen or else there is no way the attack can connect with the ground. An attack back at this moment will be absolutely effective.

What is the purpose of the stationary form?

The stationary form is an exercise whereby we stay put in a certain stance for a period of time. To some schools, this is a chi training but there is more to that. The stationary form is a supplementary training to complement the Tai Chi moving form. There are also many benefits to the stationary form like improving the sensitivity of our body parts, improving our structure and loosening up the stiff joints of the body. The other good thing about the stationary form is that it is non-dynamic. Since no movement is required, we can stay focused on communicating with our body and feeling it. If we have problem in a certain movement, it is a clever idea to perform a stationary form on that particular movement. After some training, you will find improvement to that movement. Any movements can be extracted for practice. Generally, there are no fixed rules as to how long we should stay in the stationary form. The purpose is to try to let your mind communicate with every part of your body and relax any tense areas. We can practice for a quarter to an hour if we are on the roll for the day and have plenty of time. We can practice for only three minutes if we are short on time. For beginners, it is normal for the body to feel sore in a short amount of time. It is fine to start easy and as the body gets more accustomed, increase the practice timing.

Why are we practising the form slowly?

Tai Chi originally did not start slow and relaxed. It is through the influence of the Yang style that the movements became slow and relax. Regardless of the influence, there is a benefit to training slowly. By reconstructing the body, we are trying to activate all the muscles and tendons that were long forgotten. If we move too quickly, most likely those muscles and tendons will be skipped and never be activated. Now, every movement has to be led with intent. Every movement has to split Yin Yang. Every movement has to be broken into details and done in the correct sequence. We will never achieve these if we are doing the form quickly. Practising slowly has a lot to do with feeling. Honestly, the speed of the movement differs every day. It differs even within the form itself. There are some movements that we can feel very well, and those moves will definitely make us move even slower.

Push hands

Push hands is an essential component in our Tai Chi training. The Tai Chi form is the main training component. If there is only one training that we can do in Tai Chi, we should definitely choose to practise the moving form. However, by pushing hand, we can validate the moves in our forms and refine our skills. We will improve faster. The moving form, the stationary form and the push hands should work hand in hand to improve our Tai Chi.

Some of us might have the concern for being injured while pushing hand. Push hands is not the cause of that but being competitive will definitely increase the chances of being injured. Push hands need not be competitive. It should be fun and interactive. It is not a matter of who wins or loses. As long as a person loses balance, we should stop. There is no need to make the person fall or get yourself thrown. What matters most is that we get to understand the form better through push hands and improve ourselves. We should focus on studying how to split the Yin Yang in the form and test it through push hands.

Is Tai Chi practical as a martial art?

We have seen YouTube videos of Tai Chi masters being beaten to a pulp by MMA fighters. So, is Tai Chi still practical?

This comes down to a fundamental issue – Practitioners have the wrong concept about Tai Chi.

Practitioners are often under the delusion that Tai Chi should be soft and if any strength is used, it is not Tai Chi. Practitioners are too focused on their ideal style of Tai Chi to the point that it makes Tai Chi impractical. And the sad part about this is that the practitioner thinks that he is learning the most invincible martial art on Earth and he can practically send any punks flying with a chi blast. Well, he can right if he is willing to take up the gruesome training in the good old days.

Tai Chi originally is combat martial arts. In the olden days, martial art is all about trying to kill your opponent and among all the martial arts, Tai Chi stood on the top. In fact, Tai Chi originated as a martial art that amazed the world with its supreme prowess. Founder of Yang style Yang Lu Chan was given the title "Invincible Yang" in the nineteenth century as he remains undefeated with his Tai Chi skills. This achievement made Tai Chi famous as he overwhelmed his opponents with soft movements. His opponents ranged from Chinese boxers to wrestlers and none can defeat him. Many of them were actually very impressed by his skills. From here, we can see that Tai Chi was a very practical form of martial arts. But in the current society, we are seeing something else.

Other than having delusions about Tai Chi, the other problem is that practitioners are not trained to fight. As a start, the body is not conditioned for fighting. The conditioning of the limbs is not done. Any strike to the limbs will make the practitioner go limp. The stamina is not trained. The practitioner will get out breath within a few minutes. Another point to note is that Tai Chi does not train groundwork and statistically it is very possible that a fight ends up on the ground. Without any groundwork skills, a Tai Chi practitioner will definitely lose out once he falls with the opponent to the ground. This fact has been proven by the Gracie family that practises Brazilian Jujitsu ground fighting. Anyone that does not know ground work will definitely lose the fight. In olden China, roads were full of pebbles. Therefore, the motive is to make the opponent fall hard onto the ground but never continue the fight on the ground. Groundwork cannot be developed in such an environment.

To sum it up, Tai Chi is definitely practical as a martial art, but we need to include other forms of training to make it practical. Sandbags, shin hardening, stamina building, and endless bouts of sparring have to be done. We need to be realistic and serious about sparring and not deny it since it is not soft as Tai Chi should ideally be. Lastly, no matter how good Tai Chi can be, the one using it will determine the outcome of the fight, not the martial art itself.

Conclusion

Tai Chi today is very much different from what it used to be and has evolved widely to fit the lifestyle of modern humans. Many practitioners are after the health benefits rather than the martial skills. This can be easily comprehended since we have a higher chance of getting a stiff shoulder or sore trunk than getting challenged to duel in the street.

Regardless of the reason for practising Tai Chi, it is important for the practitioner to stick to Tai Chi principles. It is important to split Yin Yang. It is important for the body to be reconstructed. We need to diligently stretch out the tendons and joints to achieve internal Tai Chi. Once the tendons are trained and joints are opened, the chi will flow, the blood will flow and the health will be better. You can be proud to say that the Tai Chi you are doing is internal. Tai Chi takes time and commitment to see results. In my opinion, this is a good thing as practitioners need not push themselves too hard till they throw up and dread training the next day. The popular martial arts today like Muay Thai or Tae Kwan Do allow the practitioner to quickly become strong in just a few months through strenuous training. Although this allows fast result, such martial arts are training the muscles more than tendons. As we all know by now, it is easy to gain muscles and also lose them. Training the tendons are a better investment. However, if you are intending to look better with nice big muscles, then this is not what tendons training can give you. Tendons trainings do not give you nice aesthetics. They just make you strong.

Another point about training the muscles is that since the movements are fast, only certain muscles are trained. And as the trained muscles become stronger, they took over the jobs of other muscles and the other muscles slowly goes dormant. Once some muscles are bigger than the other muscles, the muscles in the body become imbalanced and as soon as you stop training, pain in the body will start to show. This is inevitable as age catches up and we lose our energy, we will reduce or stop physically demanding training.

Tai Chi, on the other hand, works in the opposite manner. The movements are slow, controlled and detailed. Movements should be accurate, precise and sequenced. All movements should be coordinated but separated. To sum these all up, we just have to open our joints, train our tendons and align our posture to achieve Tai Chi. Once we can achieve all these points mentioned, we can use our body efficiently. Our bones are aligned properly to withstand attack and we can use our strength minimally. Imagine a rod that has a crack line. If we apply force on any part of the rod, the crack line will deepen and cause the rod to break. All the joints in our body are crack lines. By training the tendons and opening the joints, we are removing the crack lines. With a good structure, we are also removing these crack lines. A good structure aligns all the bones accurately so that it can withstand a large force. If any of the bones are not aligned properly, there will be a crack line in our structure. To ensure that the structure is aligned, the joints must be opened. For the joints to be opened, the tendons have to be strong and flexible. These are the secrets to internal Tai Chi. Once you achieve all these, things like health and Chi movement will fall in place. You need not look for them. They are there once you satisfy all the conditions. It might take years but that's the beauty of Tai Chi. Only the ones seeking the treasure diligently will find it. There are no such things as to be born with it or natural talent. Sure, there are some people who can achieve Tai Chi faster but we all need to train hard to achieve it. What is important is that we put our efforts into training the right things and achieving the results at the end of the day.

Author's Notes

Thank you again for downloading this book!

I hope this book is able to help you to understand Tai Chi better and improve your skills or health.

If you enjoyed this book and think it will be beneficial to others, then I'd like to ask you for a favour to leave an honest review for this book on Amazon so that other readers can decide if this is the book that is suitable for them. Very much appreciated!

Thank you, good luck and all the best!

Best Regards,

Y.W. Chen

Made in the USA
Lexington, KY
07 May 2019